EASY GUIDE TO

HIPPA
RISK ASSESSMENTS

ESSENTIAL TOOL FOR HEALTHCARE PROVIDERS

By

Lori-Ann Rickard
and
Lauren Sullivan

Presented by
Expert Health Press

ISBN-10: 1-940767-17-2

ISBN-13: 978-1-940767-17-8

For William David Rickard,
for his unwavering commitment to love and excellence.

TABLE OF CONTENTS

INTRODUCTION

Risk assessments are required under the Health Insurance and Accountability Act of 1996, better known as HIPAA.

WHAT IS *HIPAA?*

HIPAA is the federal statute that requires healthcare providers to safeguard patient identities, medical records and protected health information ("PHI"). It further requires organizations that handle PHI to regularly review the administrative, physical and technical safeguards they have in place.

Basically, HIPAA took established confidentiality healthcare practices of physicians and healthcare providers to protect patients' information and made it law.

In 2009, the Health Information Technology for Economic and Clinical Health Act ("HITECH") was enacted as part of the American Recovery and Reinvestment Act. The final rule of the HITECH Act was published in 2013 and it made significant changes to HIPAA's Privacy, Security and Enforcement rules. For example, HITECH made business associates directly liable for compliance with HIPAA Privacy and Security requirements, it expanded individuals' rights to receive electronic copies of their health information, and it restricts disclosures to a health plan concerning treatment for which the individual paid out of pocket in full. Further, HITECH modified the breach notification standards for unsecured PHI, it required modifications of Notices of Privacy Practices, and made a variety of other changes.

WHERE DO RISK ASSESSMENTS COME IN?

Risk assessments are a key requirement of complying with HIPAA. Covered entities must complete a HIPAA risk assessment to determine their risks, and protect their PHI from breaches and unauthorized access to protected information. There are many components of risk assessments, which can often seem burdensome on healthcare providers.

So, in more detail, what are risk assessments, and what do you need to do to successfully implement your organization's HIPAA risk assessment?

1

WHAT IS A HIPAA
RISK ASSESSMENT?

A HIPAA Risk Assessment is an analysis of potential risks and vulnerabilities to the confidentiality, availability and integrity of all protected health information (PHI) that the healthcare provider creates, receives, maintains, or transmits. It is the first step in getting compliant with the HIPAA Security Rule. Risk assessments help providers address their security weaknesses in an effort to prevent health data breaches or other adverse security events. Successful risk assessments also help providers avoid fines from the Office for Civil Rights (OCR) – the federal agency that is responsible for HIPAA audits and enforcement.

Complete risk assessments look at both non-electronic PHI, and electronic protected health information (e-PHI). Risk assessments ensure compliance with HIPAA's administrative, physical and technical safeguards as they are a key requirement of the HIPAA Security Rule. Further, risk assessments are a core requirement for providers seeking payment through the Medicare and Medicaid EHR Incentive Program – or the Meaningful Use Program.

An Overview

To start your risk assessment, you must first identify where PHI or e-PHI is stored, received, maintained, or transmitted. Then, you must identify and document potential risks to your PHI. You should determine the likelihood and potential impact of risks and assign a risk level ranging from high to low. Finally, you want to identify existing and necessary methods to eliminate or mitigate the risks.

Once the security risks are identified, a plan must be developed to manage and mitigate the risks found. The plan, in the form of policies and procedures, must be implemented by the provider to satisfy OCR requirements.

Many healthcare providers have HIPAA policies and procedures in place, but don't always follow them. Other providers have outdated or inadequate policies and procedures in place. These policies and procedures need to be updated regularly and implemented to avoid steep penalties and costly breaches.

Remember, if an investigator comes to your organization, they will look not only at your policies and procedures, but also at your documentation showing compliance with your policies and procedures. You will be held responsible for the details of your HIPAA policies. If your office policies are out of date or are not adequately followed, penalties will be assessed. Not following your own policies is often worse than having none at all.

HIPAA training should take place at least annually. Any and all updates require new training, and new staff must be trained upon hiring.

While a complete HIPAA Risk Assessment may sound burdensome, implementation can save your organization money. OCR fines can be costly, and breaches even more so and may result in a loss of patients.

THE BOTTOM LINE...

- A HIPAA Risk Assessment is required by the Security Rule.

- Assess and analyze potential risks and vulnerabilities to the confidentiality, availability and integrity of all protected health information.

- Develop a plan to manage and mitigate risks found in the initial portion of your organization's risk assessment.

- Update your policies and procedures regularly to adapt to changes in technology, your organization, and in the law.

- Train your staff on all of your healthcare organization's policies and procedures to avoid further security problems.

- It is important to perform a thorough risk assessment to protect your organization against potential breaches and costly OCR fines and penalties.

2

WHAT IS THE PURPOSE OF A RISK ASSESSMENT?

Risk Assessments are essential for a variety of reasons. First and foremost, they are required by the HIPAA law. Failure to implement the required policies and procedures can lead to large fines and penalties by the Office for Civil Rights – the federal agency charged with enforcing the requirements of HIPAA.

But more importantly, risk assessments can help protect your organization from a security breach and can make your patients feel secure entrusting you with their protected health information.

OCR Audits

The OCR can perform audits, whether or not your organization has had a breach. If the OCR pays your office a visit, you can expect them to do a thorough and complete audit looking for any and all areas of risk and HIPAA violations. Having a risk assessment in place with the necessary procedures adopted and followed will go a long way with the OCR. The OCR will look at your risk assessment and decide whether you are compliant or whether you are in violation and need to make changes. If you are in the latter group, having a thorough risk assessment in place will help to lower your fines and penalties. The OCR emphasizes that the way you demonstrate compliance with HIPAA is through your risk assessment.

Preparation of Employees for a Breach

Further, your risk assessment helps your organization and your staff prepare for a breach. Safeguards put into place through your risk assessment should help protect your patients' protected health information (PHI) and decrease the possibility of a breach occurring. But even if your security fails, you will be better prepared to deal with the consequences of a breach. You will have procedures in place to prepare staff for how to handle a breach so that it can be dealt with efficiently and effectively to minimize damage.

Risk assessments also help you to prepare your staff to deal with highly sensitive information. Once you have your training, you will be able to show your staff the importance of having safeguards in place and protecting information.

PREPARATION AGAINST CYBERATTACKS

The healthcare industry is a significant target of cyberattacks and it is essential that your organization adapt to fight and prevent cyber hackers.

Breaches are occurring at a more frequent basis as internet use continues to increase. Data sharing and exchange is encouraged, but at what cost to patient data?

The statistics are alarming. Every minute:

- 232 computers are infected with malware,

- 12 websites are successfully hacked,

- 416 website hacking attempts are made,

- Over 571 new websites are created, and

- 204 million emails are sent.

But more importantly, on the black market, medical records are worth $60.00, whereas credit card data sells for only $20.00. Protected health information (PHI) is clearly a significant target. Each year, cybercrime alone costs the economy $400 billion, and this cost is rising. Forty million people in the U.S. had their personal information stolen in 2013.

This is a result of the advanced nature of cybercrime and an inability to keep up on the part of the healthcare industry. Security problems are abundant. Recent industry-wide security problems include:

- Outdated technology,

- Encryption policies that are not followed, not existent or insufficient,

- Insider snooping,

- Breaches, and many additional concerns.

Given the expansive nature of hacking and the desirability of healthcare information, it is essential to adapt to threats. Firewalls were once the height of security, but now can be easily manipulated. To decrease the probability of breaches, you must perform a thorough risk assessment and determine the largest vulnerabilities of your organization's security. If you ignore these requirements, attacks are more likely and will disrupt your operations.

You need to know what threats your organization will face and how best to prevent them. For example, insider snooping is extremely problematic and can be combated through thorough pre-employment screening and training. You need to make security a priority and perform regular audits. Stay on top of your security to prevent breaches, but don't forget to prepare your employees to deal with the aftermath of a breach.

There has been some progression by way of security in the healthcare industry within the past year. For example, more health-care providers have been encrypting their data. However, other areas have gotten worse - security incidents caused by insiders are on the rise. This is why it is so important to put into place a risk assessment to prioritize your data encryption, train your employees, and protect your organization against breaches.

Your risk assessment should alert you to the biggest threats that your organization faces. It is important that you stay on top of security issues and threats so that your organization does not become part of a breach statistic.

With the increasing number and severity of breaches, HIPAA regulations, and OCR audits, ignoring your risk assessment is not an option. It is essential to protect your organization against breaches.

CYBER INSURANCE

Further, risk assessments are important because in this day and age cyber insurance is essential. Doctors and healthcare providers who deal with electronic protected health information (e-PHI) should look to further protect themselves by purchasing cyber insurance.

Cyber insurance is designed to mitigate losses from incidents, such as data breaches. This insurance is often the final step in the HIPAA risk assessment process. Most companies that offer cyber insurance require that a risk assessment be completed before insurance is issued.

Applications for cyber insurance should not be completed until you are finished implementing your risk assessment, and have policies in place to stay compliant with HIPAA. A complete risk assessment should allow you to get lower cyber insurance rates for your organization because premiums are based on your level of protection.

Cyber insurance is not only helpful after a breach, but it also reduces the number of cyber attacks by:

Encouraging healthcare providers to adopt preventative measures for more insurance coverage, and

Encouraging the implementation of policies and procedures by basing premiums on the level of self-protection a provider has in place.

Don't forget, HIPAA risk assessments are not only important to get cyber insurance, but they are essential to avoid costly OCR fines and detrimental security breaches.

THE BOTTOM LINE...

- HIPAA Risk Assessments are required.

- The OCR can perform an audit of your organization, whether or not you have experienced a breach.

- Risk assessments help you evaluate your risks to better protect you against a breach, but also prepare your organization to handle the aftermath of a breach.

- Cyber insurance can protect your organization from liability in case of a breach.

- Most cyber insurance carriers will require you to perform a risk analysis before providing coverage.

3

WHERE TO BEGIN? APPOINTING YOUR HIPAA PRIVACY AND SECURITY OFFICERS

As previously mentioned, implementation of policies and training of employees is essential, but clearly, you need to appoint someone to handle these tasks. The statute requires that both Privacy and Security Officers be appointed to carry out the nuances of your risk assessment. These officers are responsible for HIPAA compliance, and will be the primary point of contact regarding all HIPAA issues. Your Officers should be trained thoroughly on breach readiness, office protocols, and HIPAA requirements.

Staff should know who the Officers are and that they are required to report all concerns of potential violations or breaches to the officers. If the OCR performs an audit, and your staff is unable to identify your HIPAA Privacy and Security Officers, you can be sure to expect large fines.

It may be beneficial for at least one of the officers to have a background in information technology as they will be tasked with creating the inventory of devices. Further, the Officers will need to regularly review all electronic systems related to the security of e-PHI to ensure its security. The officers will also need to work closely with legal counsel to implement all required HIPAA policies and procedures.

Once they have been appointed, the Officers will be responsible for making sure the policies and procedures are followed, updated, and enforced. The Privacy and Security Officers must also determine the appropriate levels of staff access to PHI and will oversee compliance with the minimum necessary requirement for different job responsibilities. The Officers will serve as the contact person for issues regarding dissemination of PHI and getting Business Associate Agreements signed, among other things. Your HIPAA Privacy and Security Officers are also responsible for ensuring that staff are trained often and are aware of all relevant HIPAA regulations and policies.

In small offices, one person can handle the responsibilities of both the Privacy and Security Officer, however, in large offices, it may be wise to appoint multiple Officers. No matter the size of your office, it is essential that you choose well qualified individuals who are up to the task.

THE BOTTOM LINE...

- Appoint HIPAA Privacy and Security Officers to carry out your risk assessment.

- HIPAA Privacy and Security Officers are the primary point of contact for all potential breaches and HIPAA violations.

- Your staff should be well aware of who the HIPAA Privacy and Security Officers are, and should feel comfortable addressing their concerns with the Officers.

- Your HIPAA Privacy and Security Officers are responsible for creating an extensive inventory of devices. To do this, they will need to have a background in IT or be able to work closely with your IT department.

- The HIPAA Privacy and Security Officers will be responsible for ensuring your policies and procedures are current and are followed by all staff.

- Depending on the size of your organization, you may only have one person to handle all the HIPAA responsibilities, or you may need to appoint several officers if you have a large organization.

4

INVENTORY

The next step in putting your HIPAA risk assessment in place is to create an inventory of all devices used to store, access, create, or transmit PHI. To get compliant and avoid substantial OCR fines, you need to know where your PHI is stored, accessed, transmitted, and used.

To do this, it is imperative to create a complete inventory of devices at your healthcare organization. The OCR will require this inventory if your healthcare organization is audited or breached.

Inventories are especially important if your staff is able to access e-PHI on mobile devices, such as laptops, tablets and cell phones.

WHAT SHOULD BE INCLUDED IN YOUR INVENTORY?

Your inventory should be a comprehensive list of all hardware used, or that could potentially be used, to access, store or transmit PHI. For each device, the HIPAA Privacy and Security Officers should keep a list of the:

- Name of the employee(s) using the device;

- Type of the device;

- Make of the device;

- Model of the device;

- Serial number of the device; and

- Mobile Equipment Identifier (MEID) of the device, if applicable.

All hardware needs to be inventoried, including all of your organization's computers, laptops, printers, copiers, fax machines, cell phones, cameras, storage devices, tablets, etc.

Inventories must be updated regularly, and policies need to be in place that require staff members to report any and all new devices to your HIPAA Privacy and Security Officers. Staff should be trained on the importance of keeping the inventory current, and should know to report all new devices used to access PHI to the Privacy and Security Officers immediately.

If a staff member leaves your organization, there must be verification that all computer equipment, software and mobile electronic devices have been returned to avoid potential breaches and OCR fines. The HIPAA Privacy and Security Officers should have a termination checklist to follow for all employees leaving the healthcare provider.

Further, there should be safeguards in place for all mobile technology containing PHI. Not only should the information be encrypted (see Chapter 9), but you should also be able to remotely access mobile technology such as laptops so that if stolen, you can wipe the hard drive or prevent the PHI from being accessed. You should also inform employees that their devices may be monitored from time to time to ensure that they are being used appropriately. Your organization's inventory is essential to be able to remotely access and control devices. These steps can greatly mitigate damages in the face of a breach. When equipment is lost or stolen, you will need to refer to the inventory to be able to remotely wipe or shut down the device.

THE BOTTOM LINE...

- Inventories must include all devices, both personal and office-owned, that are used to access, transmit, store or create PHI.

- Inventories must be updated regularly.

- You need to make sure that you know where all the devices are located, and who has access to each device.

- Staff must be trained to report all new devices to the HIPAA Security and Privacy Officers before using the devices to access, store, transmit or create PHI.

- Your office should have an exit checklist to deal with PHI and devices when staff are terminated, quit or resign.

5

POLICIES AND PROCEDURES

Once you have a complete inventory of all hardware used to access, store or transmit protected health information (PHI), you can create the necessary policies and procedures for your health-care organization.

The HIPAA Security Rule requires healthcare providers to adopt and implement reasonable and appropriate policies and procedures. Many such policies are required under the statute, while a variety of other procedures and standards are "address-able." "Addressable" implementation specifications were developed to provide additional flexibility. Healthcare providers must decide whether the addressable policies are reasonable and appropriate to implement given the nature of their organization. If the healthcare provider does not implement the addressable specification, they must implement an equivalent alternative, if there is a reasonable and appropriate alternative.

SO WHAT TYPES OF POLICIES AND PROCEDURES ARE REQUIRED UNDER HIPAA?

Some required policies that you will need for your healthcare organization include:

- Policies on training,

- Policies on sanctions for violations,

- Policies on access of e-PHI and PHI,

- Policies regarding breaches and disaster management,

- Policies on backups and encryption, and

- Policies on social media.

Your policies and procedures should also include required forms and agreements, such as your staff Confidentiality Agreement, and your standard Business Associate Agreement which should be altered and individualized for each business associate. Your office should include policies for contingency planning, in case of a breach, and policies regarding encryption of data. There should also be policies on the physical security of PHI and e-PHI.

The OCR will inspect your organization's policies and procedures during an audit. This means that your policies and procedures must be complete and up to date to avoid severe penalties. The OCR stresses the importance of documentation, which is shown through having your policies and procedures written down and readily available and distributed to staff. It is important to start with the required policies and procedures, then add more depending on the requirements of your individual healthcare organization.

It is not enough to have adequate policies and procedures documented, they must also be followed and in place. Policies and procedures are important because they help to avoid breaches, by ensuring that proper security methods are in place. They also are essential in the face of a breach, because they instruct your staff on how to respond. Staff who have been trained thoroughly on the policies and procedures can react quickly to contain and resolve the situation if a breach does occur.

HIPAA requires these policies and procedures be reviewed periodically and updated in response to any changes that may affect the security of electronic protected health information (e-PHI). This is especially important regarding polices that cover social media and technology, as those areas are ever changing.

Generally, healthcare providers must keep their written policies and procedures for six years after the date of their creation, or their last effective date. Whichever date is later governs. This time frame may vary depending on the location of your healthcare organization.

THE BOTTOM LINE...

- There are many policies and procedures that are specifically required under HIPAA while others are not always required but are dependent on the nature of your healthcare organization.

- It is important to add additional policies and procedures that govern your organization's specific needs and address your organization's individual areas of risk.

- Train your staff thoroughly on the policies so that they can act quickly in the event of a breach.

- Include policies on contingency planning and physical safety of PHI and e-PHI.

- Have a social media policy in place to govern what your staff can say on social media and when they can access their social media accounts.

6

BUSINESS ASSOCIATE AGREEMENT

Business associates are other people and often businesses who work with the healthcare provider. The business associates may create, receive, maintain or transmit protected health information on behalf of the healthcare provider. For example, they may perform data analysis, processing or administration, billing, auditing, etc. Business Associate Agreement is a required contract between the business associate and the healthcare provider to ensure that the business associate will safeguard the healthcare provider's PHI.

While Business Associate Agreements were required before the HITECH Act was put into effect in 2013, the HITECH Act expanded the definition of a business associate and made changes to the requirements and the protections offered by these essential agreements. The HITECH Act applies directly to business associates and subcontractors. Before HITECH, business associates were only contractually liable. Since the establishment of HITECH, business associates are directly liable for breaches to the same extent as covered entities.

Covered entities can seek this liability protection ONLY if they have an updated Business Associate Agreement signed by business associate. It is essential to make sure all of your organization's agreements are updated with the requisite language extending liability to the business associates.

Business Associate Agreements are required with any business associate, and the business associate must comply with the HIPAA Security Rule standards requiring the necessary administrative, physical, and technical safeguards in place to protect PHI and e-PHI.

WHAT DO YOU NEED TO HAVE IN YOUR BUSINESS ASSOCIATE AGREEMENT?

Business Associate Agreements must establish the permitted and required uses and disclosures of PHI by the business associate. Your Agreement should provide that the business associate will not use or disclose the information other than as allowed or required by the contract, or as required by law. Business Associate Agreements must require business associates to implement appropriate safeguards to prevent the unauthorized use or disclosure of the protected information, including implementing requirements of the HIPAA Security Rule for electronic protected health information.

Further, your Agreement should require the business associate to report to the healthcare provider any use or disclosures of information that are not permitted under the Agreement, including breaches of unsecured PHI. Your business associate is required to disclose PHI as specified in its contract to satisfy your organization's obligation with respect to individuals' requests for copies of their medical records, as well as make the records available for accounting purposes. Business associates must be required to adhere to the HIPAA Privacy Rule, and make available to the U.S. Department of Health & Human Services (HHS) its internal practices, books and records relating to the use and disclosure of PHI received from the healthcare provider.

Make sure to have a provision in your Business Associate Agreement regarding termination of the Agreement, and what the business associate needs to do to return or destroy all PHI received from your organization, or created for your organization. You also need to include a provision regarding violations and breaches by the business associate.

SUBCONTRACTORS

Your agreement should also include language regarding subcontractors, as business associates can, and often do hire their own subcontractors to perform additional work. A subcontractor is defined as a person to whom a business associate delegates a function, activity or service, other than in the capacity of a member of the workforce of the business associate. The subcontractor should be held to the same standards as your business associate under your Business Associate Agreement.

A subcontractor is a business associate when that function, activity or service involves the creation, receipt, maintenance or transmission of e-PHI or PHI.

Your Business Associate Agreement should be reviewed regularly to make sure it is up to date. The agreement should be tailored to each business associate, and should include language regarding the business associate's liability, as well as any subcontractor's liability. Make sure that you have a signed agreement before allowing any business associate any access to PHI or e-PHI. Your HIPAA Privacy and Security Officers should be tasked with managing the agreements and consulting with legal counsel to update the language in the agreements periodically.

THE BOTTOM LINE...

- Business Associate Agreements are required when you do business with anyone that may have any access to your organization's e-PHI or PHI, or that will create e-PHI or PHI on behalf of your healthcare organization.

- HIPAA has been expanded by the HITECH Act which greatly affected Business Associate Agreements and obligations of business associates.

- Business Associate Agreements should be reviewed and updated regularly to ensure that your organization is getting the full protections available by law.

- Your Business Associate Agreement should also address subcontractors and subcontractors' liability.

- Make sure to have current agreements signed by all of your business associates.

- Ensure that you have a signed business associate agreement in place before allowing your business associates any access to e-PHI or PHI.

7

TRAIN YOUR EMPLOYEES

Now that you have the required HIPAA policies and procedures in place, your employees must be trained. We help our clients stay on the right side of inevitable OCR audits by making sure all employees are adequately trained on the healthcare provider's policies and procedures. You can have your HIPAA Privacy and Safety Officers train your employees, or enlist your legal counsel to train your employees.

Do not be caught off guard. The OCR will expect that your staff is fully trained on all of your organization's policies and procedures. The HIPAA Security Rule emphasizes the importance of training by requiring a security awareness and training program for your entire workforce.

Without the necessary training, your organization's policies and procedures are useless. Healthcare providers are required by the HIPAA Security Rule to ensure compliance on the part of their workforce. The way to demonstrate compliance to the OCR in the face of an audit is to train your employees. Make sure to have documentation showing the dates that your employees were trained, along with the topics on which they were trained. It is a good idea to have employees sign in on a training log with the date and a brief summary of the training.

It is also often helpful to encourage staff to take notes or provide handouts that they can refer to later on after the training has ended.

WHEN IS TRAINING NECESSARY?

At least annually;

- Any time your policies or procedures are updated; and

- New employees must be trained upon joining your healthcare organization.

In the case of an audit, the OCR will expect to see documentation of your HIPAA trainings. We help our clients meet this obligation by providing them with training logs and outlines after we complete their security awareness and training program. Staff members should also receive copies or have access to the healthcare provider's policies and procedures.

Not only is training required by the OCR, but sufficient training will help your organization to mitigate potential security breaches and to mitigate any damages from breaches that do occur.

BUT WHY IS IT SO IMPORTANT TO TRAIN YOUR EMPLOYEES?

Statistically speaking - your employees are the biggest threat to the security of your organization's PHI and e-PHI. While outside breaches are extremely prevalent, most security breaches are not caused by cyberattacks or unencrypted devices. Most breaches are the result of internal employees.

Employee negligence is the leading cause of security lapses. In fact, employee negligence accounts for 37% of healthcare provider security issues.

Other causes of security breaches include:

- Theft of devices (22%);

- Employee theft (16%);

- Malware (14%); and

- Phishing scams (11%).

These statistics show that employees are a fundamental part of your breach readiness plan, as they account for 53% of security incidents.

SO HOW CAN YOU PREVENT BREACHES
CAUSED BY EMPLOYEE NEGLIGENCE AND THEFT?

It is essential to have adequate security policies and procedures in place. Your policies and procedures should be thorough, and include adequate sanctions for employee negligence and theft.

Next, it is important to educate your employees. Training employees on your policies, procedures, and breach readiness can help to reinforce the importance of security and the consequences for failure to comply. It is important that your employees know how important security is to your organization. The tone must be set from the beginning. Make sure your senior staff is in compliance and sets good examples for newer employees. Your HIPAA Privacy and Security Officer should teach employees to be "HIPAA police" and to report violations to the Officers, and remind each other of the importance of following the healthcare provider's policies and procedures.

Further, it is also essential to put security measures in place with detection capabilities. Know when your employees are accessing records and make sure to include all devices in your risk assessment inventory. Adequate training and enforcement of policies can help your healthcare organization avoid or mitigate a breach at the hands of an employee.

CAN ADEQUATE TRAINING REDUCE INSIDER SNOOPING B
Y YOUR HEALTHCARE ORGANIZATION'S EMPLOYEES?

It can. Many healthcare providers are victims to insider snooping by their employees. Unauthorized access by employees into patient records is a big deal with harsh consequences. Insider snooping leads to costly compliance issues, large OCR fines, and loss of patient trust.

There is always a risk of unauthorized access, but you can implement initiatives to make sure it doesn't happen at your healthcare organization. The best way to prevent employees inappropriately looking at e-PHI or PHI is to take proactive measures, starting with training all of your staff thoroughly. Employees should be fully aware of the consequences of looking at the records to which they do not have access. Your policies should cover regular trainings and consequences. Maintain prevention efforts by performing your own audits and making employees aware of audits during training sessions.

Training should include relevant instruction about the importance of patient privacy. New employees should also be taught about their responsibilities and expectations regarding patient privacy. We help our clients train their employees and their privacy officers to prevent unauthorized access of patient records. We also assist them in educating their employees about the consequences of internal snooping. It is often helpful for your HIPAA Privacy and Security Officers to work closely with your legal team to train employees so that the employees are trained properly and understand the importance of the HIPAA training.

It is also important to create a workplace culture that embraces privacy and security. One way to reinforce this is to have periodic reminders sent out by your organization's HIPAA Privacy and Security Officers and periodic training. Internal audits are also necessary to demonstrate that the HIPAA training is working.

Your employees should be aware that unauthorized access into patient medical records is a serious offense, and that your organization takes unauthorized access very seriously. Prevention of internal snooping requires constant efforts on the part of your HIPAA Privacy and Security Officers, and a serious investment by your organization.

HIPAA preparedness is a perpetual task that constantly changes with new technology and data-sharing requirements – many of which did not exist when the rules were finalized.

WORKFORCE CONFIDENTIALITY AGREEMENTS

Part of your employee training should include having your staff sign confidentiality agreements. Your confidentiality agreements should be distributed upon hiring new employees and should include a description of the PHI and e-PHI that they may encounter. It should inform them that they must maintain the confidentiality of all PHI. Further, it should inform them that they may not access any more PHI than is minimally required by their job description.

The confidentiality agreements should also stress that employees are not to discuss any patient information with each other in areas where unauthorized individuals may hear such information, such as in hallways, elevators, public transportation, restaurants or at social gatherings.

Your confidentiality agreement should further require employees to refrain from making unauthorized transmissions, copies, disclosures, photographs, videos, audio recordings, inquiries or modifications of any PHI.

Sanctions for violations of the confidentiality agreement should be clearly spelled out and should include termination, as well as potential liability and penalties.

Employees should be required to have unique passwords to log in to any and all servers that contain e-PHI. They should not be permitted to share their passwords with anyone, and should not write them down in places where they are visible to others.

Employees should sign and date the confidentiality agreement. Make sure that your organization retains the originals of the executed confidentiality agreements.

THE BOTTOM LINE...

- Training your employees is an essential part of your HIPAA risk assessment and should not be taken lightly.

- You should train all new employees of your organization upon their hire.

- Continue to train your employees often and regularly, at least once per year, and whenever your policies are updated.

- Significant training can help you minimize the problems created from employees.

- Train your employees to avoid unauthorized snooping into patient care records.

- Make sure your employees know who the HIPAA Privacy and Security Officers are so that they can report any violations or breaches immediately.

8

AUDITS

The OCR performs audits of healthcare providers regularly, and the number of audits is increasing. The OCR has the power to issue large fines and penalties for failure to have the required policies and procedures in place, even when no breach has occurred. Some providers have been issued penalties of over $1 million dollars when no PHI or e-PHI was ever exposed. HIPAA audits are even being conducted on business associates that are not covered entities. The OCR is auditing small and large healthcare providers to ensure compliance so it is essential that your organization is prepared when the OCR shows up. The OCR has stated that healthcare providers will have only two weeks to respond to a data request and that all information must be current as of the date of the request.

The OCR will review your policies and procedures, see how they are implemented, review your workforce training documentation, and look at all incident responses. The OCR will investigate how your organization identifies breaches or security threats, and how you respond and mitigate threats or breaches. It will also look to see what sanctions were issued if your employees played a part in any threat or breach.

Prepare your healthcare organization by first performing internal audits of your data and creating an audit log. You should have an audit log in place to make sure you know who is accessing PHI.

Audit logs are vital for recognizing inappropriate access to patient charts. They can identify when very important person ("VIP") patient records (i.e., board members, celebrities, governmental or community figures, physician providers, management staff, or other highly publicized individuals) are accessed; identify when patient files are accessed after no activity for 120 days; and identify when patients' files are accessed by employees or workstations that should not have access to said files (ex. scheduler accessing a relative's PHI). Once you have performed your own audit of your organization by looking at your patient charts, access of e-PHI and PHI, your policies and procedures, your training and your incident response procedures, it is wise to hire an outside company to perform a regular audit of your organization.

Outside audits are essential to get a better picture of your organization's security and privacy. They will also make sure that you are in compliance with your payments. Audits are often viewed as a way to improve your organization and the security of your data. Outside companies will be able to take an unbiased look at your healthcare organization and may make a difference in the security of your organization's PHI. Remember it is wise to have all outside companies retained by your healthcare lawyer so that the results can be protected.

THE BOTTOM LINE...

- The OCR has stated that they are performing more and more healthcare audits of both covered entities and business associates.

- The OCR will look through everything your healthcare organization has to offer, and will issue hefty fines if they find your policies, procedures and documentation to be lacking.

- Prepare your organization by first performing an internal audit.

- Hire an outside company, through your healthcare attorney, to do an audit of your company for unbiased results and a better picture of what is really going on inside your healthcare organization.

- Audits can help prepare you for the OCR and can help prevent and detect breaches of PHI and e-PHI.

9

BREACHES AND BREACH READINESS

Breaches are becoming more prevalent and more problematic throughout the healthcare industry. Patient and healthcare provider data is constantly at risk. Once you have put your policies and procedures in place, you need to follow through. You should have adequate policies that cover breaches and breach readiness. Breaches are the impermissible use or disclosure that compromises the security or privacy of PHI or e-PHI.

The Final Rule of HIPAA broadens the definition of breach of unsecured PHI and states that an impermissible use or disclosure of PHI is presumed to be a breach, unless there is a demonstration that there is a low probability that the PHI was compromised.

There are three exceptions to the definition of "breach." The first exception applies to the unintentional acquisition, access, or use of protected health information by a workforce member or person acting under the authority of a covered entity or business associate, if such acquisition, access, or use was made in good faith and within the scope of authority. The second exception applies to the inadvertent disclosure of protected health information by a person authorized to access protected health information at a covered entity or business associate to another person authorized to access protected health information at the covered entity or business associate, or organized health care arrangement in which the covered entity participates. In both cases, the information cannot be further used or disclosed in a manner not permitted by the Privacy Rule.

The final exception applies if the covered entity or business associate has a good faith belief that the unauthorized person to whom the impermissible disclosure was made, would not have been able to retain the information.

The key to protecting your organization is to be smarter about your security methods and aware of breach trends. Preparing for breaches can be a daunting task. Hackers often seem to be one step ahead of the latest security measures.

So how can your healthcare organization prevent a breach?

First, you should be aware of the three main areas of concern for healthcare organizations. They are:

- Physical theft/loss;

- Insider misuse; and

- Miscellaneous errors.

Almost half (46%) of security incidents result from loss of information assets such as laptops, hard drives and paper files. It is important for you to make sure your HIPAA Risk Assessment deals with lost or stolen items. It is essential that you prepare tailored policies and procedures to deal with your specific equipment and data.

To protect your data and mitigate your risk from breaches you need to train your staff. Carelessness on the part of your staff can lead to many breaches. Routine training is essential to enforce the importance of mindfulness within your healthcare organization. You should also make sure all data is backed up regularly and only on your work server.

Finally, to prevent physical theft or loss of your data, lock it up. Keep all paper files locked up in file cabinets. Lock office doors and make sure all computers and laptops have layers of unique password protections.

You are responsible for discovering breaches and you need to act without delay. You will be better prepared if you have policies in place that your staff takes seriously. One essential policy to put in place is an encryption policy.

ENCRYPTION

In today's world of breaches and cyber hacking, it is essential to encrypt all PHI when possible. It is becoming easier and more accessible for healthcare providers to encrypt their data because of advances in technology.

Encryption is the use of an algorithmic process to transform data into a form in which there is a low probability of assigning meaning without the use of a confidential process or key. This basically means if you encrypt your data, even if it is hacked, the hacker will not be able to read the data without a code or key to access the information.

If your data is encrypted, lost and stolen assets are much less damaging to your healthcare organization. Your HIPAA Privacy and Security Officers should, on a periodic and routine basis, meet with the appropriate parties, such as management, information technology professionals, software vendors, legal counsel, and others to encrypt all e-PHI that your organization creates, receives, maintains or transmits.

It would also be beneficial to convert all paper and hard copy PHI into an electronic format and then secure it consistent with your organization's encryption policy and procedures. Paper or other hard copy PHI should be scanned or otherwise converted into digital format, then the original hard copy can be destroyed in a manner that ensures the PHI cannot be read or reconstructed. If your healthcare organization enters into an agreement with a company to shred your PHI, don't forget to have that company sign your Business Associate Agreement.

It is advisable to have all e-PHI encrypted, and to have encryption keys stored in different locations than the data which it is meant to decrypt.

THE BOTTOM LINE...

- Breaches are occurring more frequently and in many different ways.

- Familiarize yourself and your office with breach trends so that you can stay on top of your office security.

- The Final Rule of HIPAA expanded the definition of breaches and states that any impermissible use or disclosure of PHI is presumed to be a breach, unless there is a demonstration that there is a low probability that the PHI was compromised.

- Be smart about your security systems and stay on top of your breach readiness program.

- Lock up all of your PHI and make sure to know where all of your information is stored, and who can access your PHI.

- Encrypt all of your e-PHI and convert your PHI to an electronic format so that you can encrypt that too.

10

WHAT TO DO AFTER A BREACH

It is imperative that your healthcare organization responds immediately after becoming aware that a breach has occurred. While it is essential, and required, that you put a thorough risk assessment and measures in place to prevent a breach, it is important to remember that no healthcare organization is immune from a data breach. How your organization responds to a breach is just as important as how you prepare to prevent a breach.

The chances of your organization facing a breach are likely given recent events. The statistics regarding breaches are overwhelming. In the past two years:

- 91% of healthcare organizations have had a data breach;

- 39% of healthcare organizations have had two to five breaches; and

- 40% of healthcare organizations have had more than five breaches.

Malicious attacks, such as cyber attacks and insider snooping, are up a whopping 125% since 2010. Cases of medical identity theft have nearly doubled in the past five years to over 2.3 million victims in 2014. These breaches are costing the healthcare industry $6 billion per year, and could greatly impact your organization. It is important to include thorough guidelines in your HIPAA Risk Assessment as to what your employees should do after a breach.

Breaches can lead to not only a loss of data, but also a loss of patients along with hefty fines and sanctions. It is important to train your staff on how to deal with a breach and put extensive guidelines in place. Know that you will face questions from patients and be prepared with answers.

Following the right steps in the aftermath of a breach can potentially save your healthcare organization.

You need to start by mitigating your damages after a breach. The Privacy Rule requires healthcare providers to mitigate, to the extent practicable, the harmful effects of uses or disclosures that violate its privacy policies or the HIPAA Privacy Rule.

The HIPAA Security Rule requires healthcare providers to mitigate, to the extent practicable, harmful effects of security incidents as well. Mitigation includes retrieving or limiting the further distribution of impermissibly used or disclosed information and notifying the affected individuals of the violation. This is especially important when the individual needs to take self-proactive measures to avoid further harm.

You should make sure that your healthcare organization documents the security incident, an extensive analysis of the incident, as well as the actions that were taken to mitigate the harm. Further document all corrective actions taken by your organization. If you do not take certain corrective actions, document your explanation as to why.

Determine if you need to report the breach under the Breach Notification Rule. The discovery clock starts ticking when the breach is known or when the breach would have become known if reasonable diligence was exercised. Stay in tune with your organization because if your employees know of a breach, that knowledge is attributed to the healthcare provider or business associate. Your HIPAA Privacy and Security Officers must stay in touch and available to employees so that they learn of any breaches quickly.

Business Associates must notify covered entities without unreasonable delay, and in no case may they notify later than 60 days after discovery of the breach.

Breach notifications are not required if there is a low probability that the PHI was compromised. A covered entity or business associate must now undertake a four-factor risk assessment to determine whether or not PHI has been compromised and it must overcome the presumption that the breach must be reported. The four-factor risk assessment focuses on:

1. The nature and extent of the PHI involved in the incident (e.g., whether the incident involved sensitive

information like social security numbers or infectious disease test results);

2. The recipient of the PHI;

3. Whether the PHI was actually acquired or viewed; and

4. The extent to which the risk that the PHI was compromised has been mitigated following unauthorized disclosure (e.g., whether it was immediately sequestered and destroyed).

If an evaluation of the four factors fails to demonstrate that there is a low probability that the PHI has been compromised, then notification is required. It is likely that more unauthorized uses and disclosures of PHI will be required to be reported to affected individuals and to the OCR.

If under the four-factor test your organization does need to notify individuals of a breach, you must provide notification to individuals without unreasonable delay, and no later than 60 calendar days after discovery. **CAUTION: You should never perform this four-part analysis without the advice of a healthcare lawyer.**

Failure to mitigate your damages and failure to notify individuals will lead to costly fines from the OCR that most healthcare providers cannot afford. If you purchase cyber insurance as part of your risk assessment, you will be better off in the face of a breach. Cyber insurance is designed to mitigate losses from cyber incidents, including data breaches.

Stay proactive in your approaches so that your staff is trained and your policies are updated. This will ensure a better response after a breach occurs, lower fines from the OCR, and a better chance of surviving a breach and retaining your patients.

THE BOTTOM LINE...

- With the increase in breaches, chances are your healthcare organization will face a breach or security incident of some kind.

- It is important to prepare your organization with a complete risk assessment to prevent breaches, but also to address how your employees should respond after a breach has occurred.

- Determine whether you need to notify individuals based on an analysis using the four-part notification test.

- Mitigate your damages as quickly as possible after discovery of a breach.

- Make sure your staff are trained for what to do after a breach, and are trained to notify your HIPAA Privacy and Security Officers immediately upon discovery of a breach.

- Stay proactive to prevent a loss of your patients and hefty fines from the OCR.

- Consult your healthcare attorney.

Conclusion

Breaches are not going away, in fact they are happening more often. For the safety of your organization, you need to put into place a thorough HIPAA Risk Assessment. Risk assessments are essential, not only to protect your healthcare organization from breaches, but also to comply with HIPAA and to prepare for an OCR audit. Without a complete risk assessment and adequate policies and procedures in place, your organization will likely pay severe penalties and fines.

To complete your HIPAA Risk Assessment, start by appointing HIPAA Privacy and Security Officers. Have them, along with your legal counsel and IT department, prepare an inventory of devices to identify where PHI is stored, received, maintained or transmitted. Then identify and document all potential risks to your PHI. Determine the likelihood of the risks, as well as the potential impact so that you can assign levels for the risks. Finally, identify existing and necessary methods to mitigate the risks. This includes updating your policies and procedures and performing audits. Once this is done, train your employees.

Once you have completed your risk assessment, appointed your HIPAA Privacy and Security Officers, completed your inventory, have your policies and procedures in place, it is important to follow through with regular updates and routine trainings.

If you do experience a breach, know what you need to do to mitigate your damage and notify affected individuals. The more prepared you are, the better chance your organization has of avoiding OCR fines and breaches.

Terms to Know

Audit: The systematic review and evaluation of records and other data to determine the quality of the services or products provided, or the compliance with applicable laws. Providers should perform internal audits, as well as hire an outside company (through counsel) to perform an audit to ensure compliance with HIPAA.

Breach: An impermissible use or disclosure under the HIPAA Privacy Rule that compromises the security or privacy of protected health information. An impermissible use or disclosure of protected health information is presumed to be a breach unless the covered entity or business associate demonstrates there is a low probability that the protected health information has been compromised.

Business Associate: A person or entity, other than a member of the workforce of a healthcare provider, who performs functions or activities on behalf of or provides services to a healthcare provider. These services or functions involve access to protected health information.

Business Associate Agreement: A required contract between a healthcare provider and a business associate that is used to safeguard protected health information by limiting and clarifying the permissible uses and disclosures of protected health information by the business associate.

Covered Entity: A health plan, a health care clearinghouse or a health provider who transmits any health information in electronic form in connection with a transaction covered by HIPAA.

Cyber Insurance: Coverage for liability that arises out of the unauthorized use or access to electronic protected health information within your organization. It can also provide coverage for liability claims for the spread of a virus, computer theft, extortion, or a mistake made by your employees.

Electronic Protected Health Information (e-PHI): Any electronic information about health status, provision of health care or payment of health care that can be linked to a specific individual. It is interpreted broadly and it includes names, Social Security Numbers, addresses, birthdays, etc.

Encryption: A method for protecting electronic data in which the sender provides a key to the recipient so only that recipient can view the data.

Health Insurance Portability and Accountability Act (HIPAA): U.S. federal law governing how the healthcare industry should maintain the privacy and security of individually identifiable health information. (45 CFR Part 160 et seq.)

HIPAA Privacy and Security Officers: The employees appointed to oversee all activities related to the development, implementation and maintenance of your HIPAA policies and procedures. They are the primary point of contact for all HIPAA related issues, including breaches and violations.

HIPAA Privacy Rule: This portion of the HIPAA statute protects the privacy of individually identifiable health information held by covered entities and their business associates and gives patients rights to their information. (45 CFR Part 160; 45 CFR Part 164 A, E)

HIPAA Security Rule: This portion of the HIPAA statute sets national standards for the security of electronic health information. It specifies a series of administrative, physical, and technical safeguards for covered entities and their business associates to use to assure the confidentiality, integrity and availability of e-PHI. (45 CFR Part 160; 45 CFR Part 164 A, C)

Information Technology for Economic and Clinical Health Act (HITECH): Expansion of HIPAA that covers electronic health information and expands the privacy protections given to patients.

Inventory: A comprehensive list of all hardware used, or that could potentially be used, to access, store or transmit PHI or e-PHI. This list must be updated regularly so that your HIPAA Privacy and Security Officers know where all the devices are at all times.

Office for Civil Rights (OCR): The federal government agency tasked with enforcing HIPAA. (http://www.hhs.gov/ocr/office/index.html)

Protected Health Information (PHI): Any information about health status, provision of healthcare or payment of health care that can be linked to a specific individual. It is interpreted broadly and it includes names, Social Security Numbers, addresses, birthdays, etc.

Risk Assessment: An analysis of potential risks and vulnerabilities to the confidentiality, availability and integrity of all protected health information (PHI) that the healthcare provider creates, receives, maintains, or transmits.

DISCLAIMER

No part of this publication may be reproduced, stored in a retrieval system or transmitted in any form or by any means, electronic, mechanical, photocopying, recording, scanning or otherwise, without the prior permission of the publisher.

The publisher and the author make no representations or warranties with respect to the accuracy or completeness of the contents of this work and specifically disclaim all warranties, including without limitation warranties of fitness for a particular purpose. No warranty may be created or extended by sales or promotional materials. The advice and strategies contained herein may not be suitable for every situation. This work is sold with the understanding that the publisher is not engaged in rendering legal, medical, or other professional advice or services. If professional assistance is required, the services of a competent professional person should be sought. Neither the publisher nor the author shall be liable for damages arising here from. The fact that an organization or website is referred to in this work as a citation and/or a potential source of further information does not mean that the author or the publisher endorses the information the organization or website may provide or recommendations it may make. Further, readers should be aware that the internet websites listed in this work may have changed or disappeared between when this work was written and when it is read. This book is provided for informational purposes only. Following the contents within this book does not guarantee compliance with federal, state or local laws. Please note that this information may not be applicable or appropriate for all healthcare providers and organizations. This is not an exhaustive source on safeguarding health information from privacy and security risks.

We encourage you to consult with your healthcare attorney when performing your HIPAA Risk Assessment.

RICKARD & ASSOCIATES IS ON YOUR SIDE

"When I need legal health care advice and answers, I call Rickard & Associates. They are efficient, thorough and extremely knowledgeable!"

M. Diane Vogt, JD

"Rickard & Associates are my 'go-to' experts on healthcare law. They make it understandable and easy to follow for our doctors and their patients, too."

Michele Nichols, The Physician Alliance

"Rickard & Associates knows the healthcare system and the legal system, inside and out. Whenever we have questions about health-care, Rickard & Associates has the answers."

Mike Gerstenlauer, St. John -Macomb Hospital

"Whenever my family has a legal or health care issue, Rickard & Associates is my first call for the best advice, advocates, and answers."

Donna Curran

"Getting a lawyer that is willing to advocate for you on tough, healthcare issues is never easy, unless you call Rickard & Associates. Rickard & Associates can answer all your legal questions!"

Coreen Buehrer

"Lori-Ann has a unique, inside perspective of the healthcare system. She knows how to be proactive and get things done. No other law firm will help you navigate the bewildering maze of hospitals, multiple specialists and insurance companies like Rickard & Associates will."

John Mallender, Office Manager of Large Physician Practice

ABOUT THE AUTHORS

LORI-ANN RICKARD

Lori-Ann Rickard, J.D., CPC, CAC, is one of the country's top healthcare lawyers. Ms. Rickard founded Rickard & Associates, P.C. in 2000 after many years as a partner at a large Detroit law firm, and later as corporate counsel for the St. John Providence Health System, a member of Ascension Health. Ms. Rickard is an accomplished litigator and experienced corporate attorney. She is a recognized leader in the ever-changing field of healthcare law. Ms. Rickard is a nationally known public speaker and published author of many books and articles on healthcare matters. She has been honored by Best Lawyers and DB Business "Top Lawyers." With clients ranging from national healthcare systems, ambulance companies and medical vendors to all types of physicians, Ms. Rickard combines cutting edge legal knowledge with the desire to help clients reach intelligent, practical legal solutions that meet their unique needs.

LAUREN SULLIVAN

Lauren Sullivan is an associate attorney at Rickard & Associates, P.C. where she provides a broad range of litigation and transactional services for corporations and individuals. She focuses her practice on general business matters with a specialty in representing physicians and health care practices. As a specialist in health care law and related regulations, Ms. Sullivan frequently advises clients regarding physician/practice/hospital regulations, privacy and security and HIPAA risk assessments. Ms. Sullivan has represented clients in many criminal and civil issues throughout the state of Michigan.